Community Helpers During COVID-19

Food Workers During COVID-19

Robin Johnson

CRABTREE
PUBLISHING COMPANY
WWW.CRABTREEBOOKS.COM

CRABTREE
PUBLISHING COMPANY
WWW.CRABTREEBOOKS.COM

Author: Robin Johnson
Series research and development:
Janine Deschenes
Editorial director: Kathy Middleton
Editor: Janine Deschenes
Proofreader: Melissa Boyce
Graphic design: Katherine Berti
Image research: Robin Johnson
Print coordinator: Katherine Berti

Images:
Alamy
    National Guard: p. 6 (bottom)
    Pacific Press Media Production Corp: p. 16 (bottom)
    Sipa USA: p. 11 (bottom)
Getty Images
    China News Service: p. 17 (top)
Istockphoto
    Bobby Coutu: p. 10 (bottom)
Shutterstock
    5D Media: p. 5
    Chadolfski: p. 18 (bottom)
    Deeper Look Photography: p. 19 (bottom)
    F. Armstrong Photography: p. 11 (top)
    John and Penny: p. 8
    Melting Spot: p. 4 (bottom)
    Mike Dotta: p. 23 (top right)
    Noushad Thekkayil: front cover
    Steve Skjold: p. 7 (top)
All other images by Shutterstock

Library and Archives Canada Cataloguing in Publication

Title: Food workers during COVID-19 / Robin Johnson.
Names: Johnson, Robin (Robin R.), author.
Description: Series statement: Community helpers during COVID-19 |
    Includes index.
Identifiers: Canadiana (print) 20200390821 |
    Canadiana (ebook) 20200390848 |
    ISBN 9781427128324 (hardcover) |
    ISBN 9781427128362 (softcover) |
    ISBN 9781427128409 (HTML)
Subjects: LCSH: COVID-19 (Disease)–Juvenile literature. |
    LCSH: Food service employees–Juvenile
 literature. | LCSH: Epidemics–Social aspects–Juvenile literature. |
    LCSH: Community life–Juvenile literature.
Classification: LCC RA644.C67 J642 2021 | DDC j614.5/92414–dc23

Library of Congress Cataloging-in-Publication Data

Available at the Library of Congress

Crabtree Publishing Company
www.crabtreebooks.com   1-800-387-7650

Printed in the U.S.A./012021/CG20201112

Published in Canada
Crabtree Publishing
616 Welland Ave.
St. Catharines, Ontario
L2M 5V6

Published in the United States
Crabtree Publishing
347 Fifth Ave.
Suite 1402-145
New York, NY 10016

Published in the United Kingdom
Crabtree Publishing
Maritime House
Basin Road North, Hove
BN41 1WR

Published in Australia
Crabtree Publishing
Unit 3 - 5 Currumbin Court
Capalaba
QLD 4157

Contents

What Is COVID-19?

COVID-19 is a **disease** that began to make people sick in 2019. It spread quickly from person to person. Soon there was a **pandemic**. It spread all around the world.

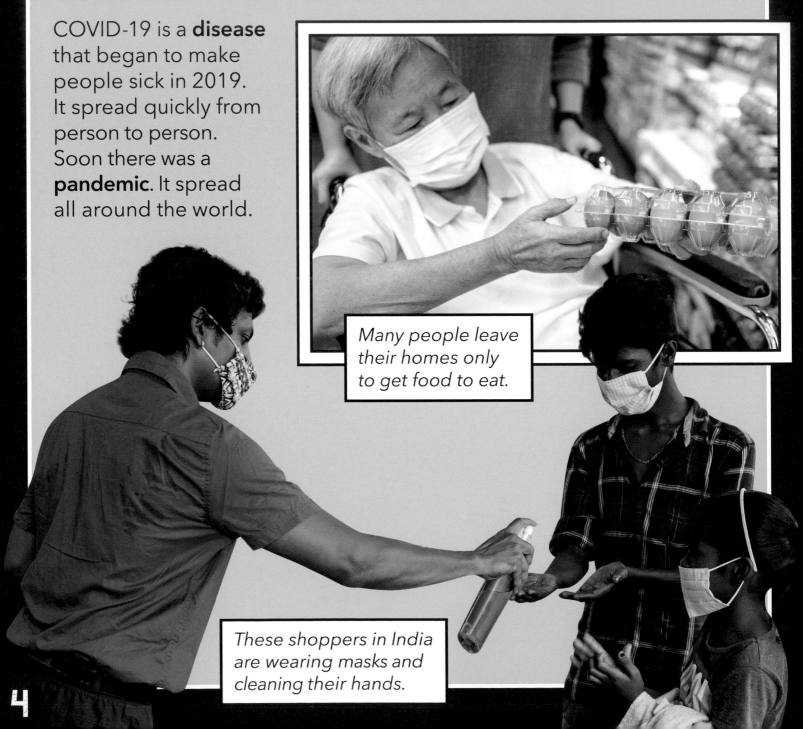

Many people leave their homes only to get food to eat.

These shoppers in India are wearing masks and cleaning their hands.

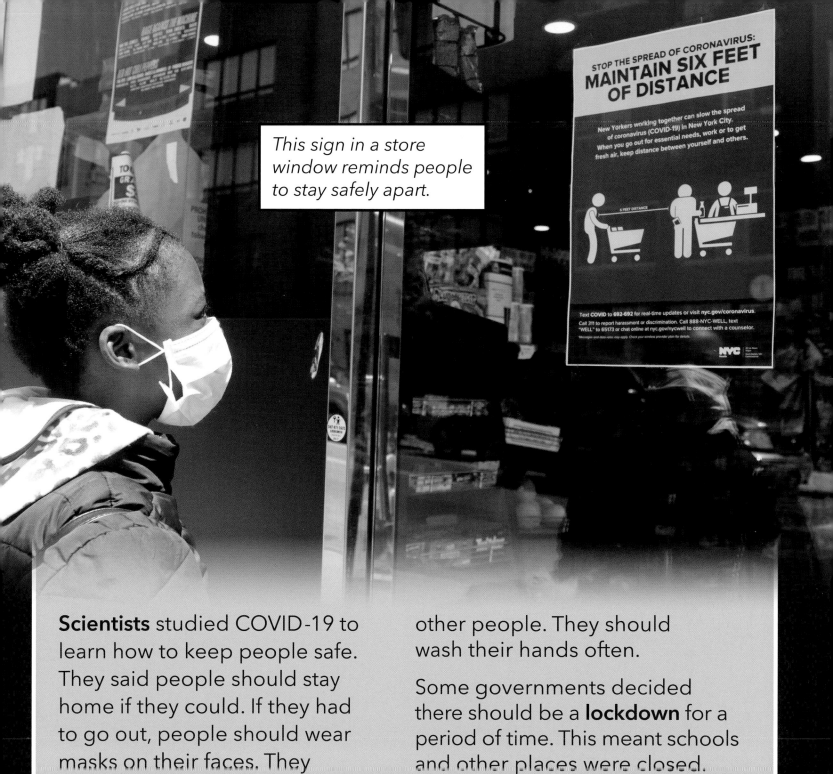

This sign in a store window reminds people to stay safely apart.

STOP THE SPREAD OF CORONAVIRUS:
MAINTAIN SIX FEET OF DISTANCE

New Yorkers working together can slow the spread of coronavirus (COVID-19) in New York City. When you go out for essential needs, work or to get fresh air, keep distance between yourself and others.

Text **COVID** to 692-692 for real-time updates or visit nyc.gov/coronavirus.

Call 311 to report harassment or discrimination. Call 888-NYC-WELL, text "WELL" to 65173 or chat online at nyc.gov/nycwell to connect with a counselor.

Scientists studied COVID-19 to learn how to keep people safe. They said people should stay home if they could. If they had to go out, people should wear masks on their faces. They should not get too close to other people. They should wash their hands often.

Some governments decided there should be a **lockdown** for a period of time. This meant schools and other places were closed. People were told to stay home.

5

Community Helpers

People work together to keep their communities safe. A community is a group of people who live, work, and play in a place. Helpers in each community make sure everyone's needs are met.

These helpers are packing fruits and vegetables for people in their community.

*Some workers bring **groceries** right out to people's cars.*

All people have a **basic need** for food. During the pandemic, workers have made sure people can get the food they need. They bravely work in stores, restaurants, farms, and other places. They bring food to people in new ways.

Grocery Store Workers

Many people get most of their food at grocery stores. Grocery store workers have made sure this is still possible during the pandemic. They keep food and other supplies on the shelves. They help keep shoppers safe.

Many grocery stores added shields to their checkout counters. The shields keep workers and shoppers safely apart.

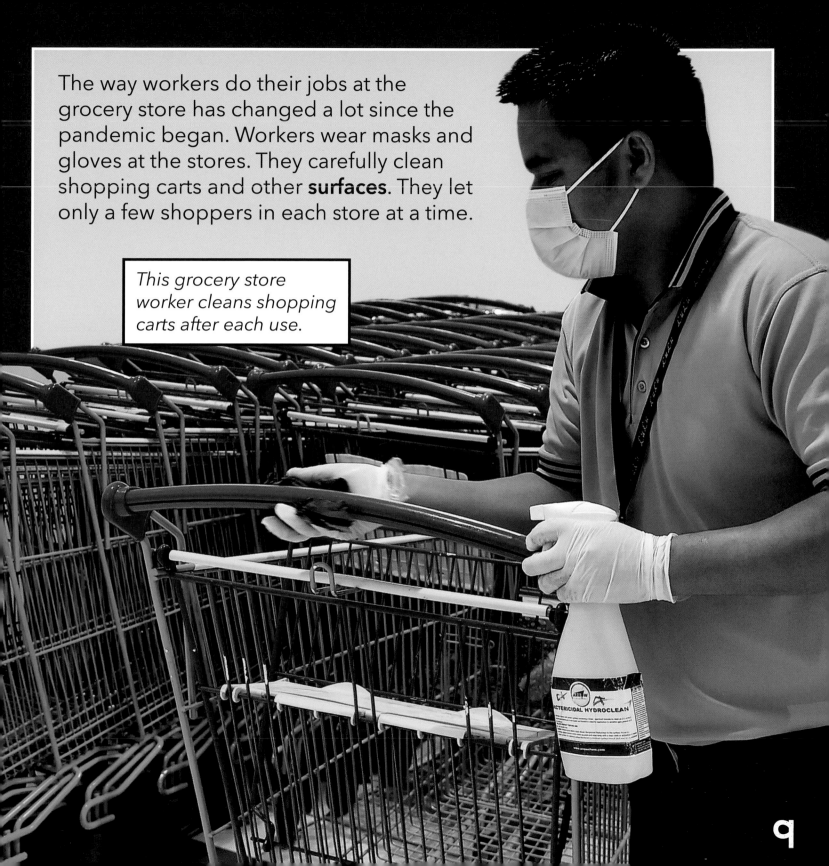

The way workers do their jobs at the grocery store has changed a lot since the pandemic began. Workers wear masks and gloves at the stores. They carefully clean shopping carts and other **surfaces**. They let only a few shoppers in each store at a time.

This grocery store worker cleans shopping carts after each use.

Cooks and Restaurant Workers

Restaurant workers make food for people to eat during the pandemic. During lockdowns, dining rooms were closed. People could still pick up food or get it delivered, however.

These cooks are working together to make tasty meals.

These workers are taking orders outside. They are keeping a safe distance from customers.

Workers also make food in hospitals, hotels, jails, and other places. Cooks in every kitchen wear masks. They wash their hands often. They keep their kitchens and cooking tools very clean.

This cook is making food for people at a hospital.

Food Producers

Many people are **stocking up** on food during the pandemic. They buy foods that last a long time, such as soup. Food **producers** work hard to make enough food for everyone.

This food worker helps produce bottled water.

This food worker bakes many loaves of bread each day.

Food producers wear masks and gloves at work. Some wear jackets or suits for safety. They stay away from other workers. They carefully clean the tools and machines they use to make food.

This worker is carefully cleaning a rack that holds baked foods.

Farmers

Farmers are growing fresh food for people to eat during the pandemic. They grow fruits and vegetables. They raise animals for their meat, milk, and eggs. Many people want to buy these fresh foods to stay healthy.

Farm workers stay apart when they pick crops in fields.

14

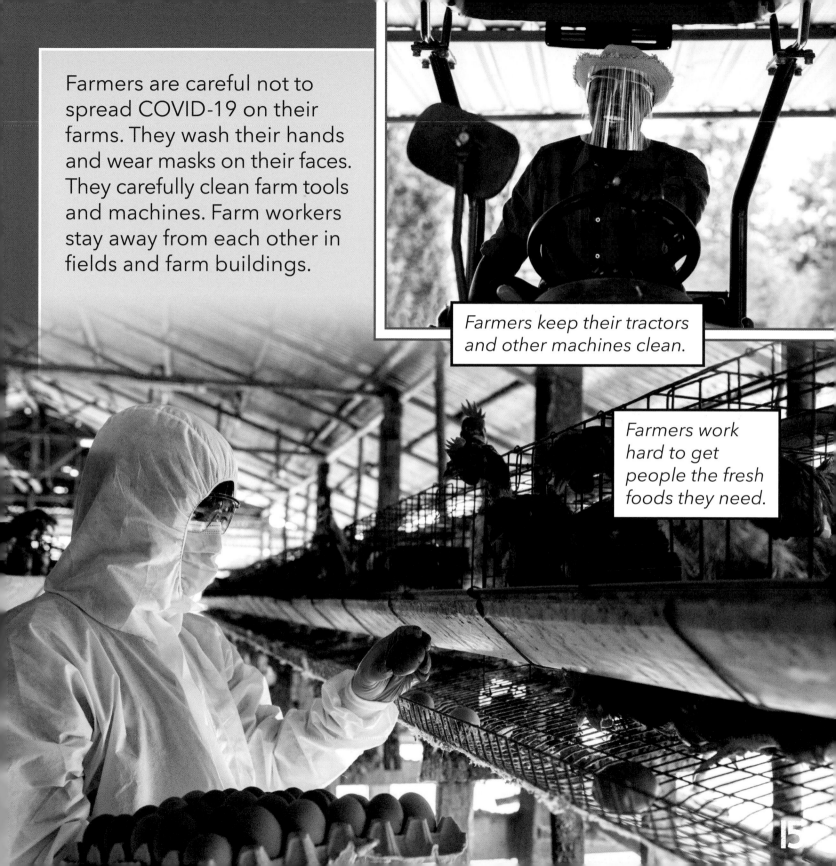

Farmers are careful not to spread COVID-19 on their farms. They wash their hands and wear masks on their faces. They carefully clean farm tools and machines. Farm workers stay away from each other in fields and farm buildings.

Farmers keep their tractors and other machines clean.

Farmers work hard to get people the fresh foods they need.

Hunters and Fishers

Some people catch food to feed people in their communities. Hunters catch deer, turkeys, and other wild animals. They fill their freezers with fresh meat without going to grocery stores.

This hunter is searching for ducks to catch.

This worker is cleaning the dock near a fishing boat.

Fishers caught these fish. Now food producers are putting the fish into cans. Canned fish has been popular during the pandemic because it lasts a long time.

This shopper is buying fish in a grocery store. A fisher caught the fish for her to eat.

Other people catch fish to eat. They carefully clean their fishing gear and boats. They deliver fresh fish to homes. Fishers also sell fish to restaurants, grocery stores, and food producers.

Food Delivery People

Truck drivers work long hours to bring people the food they need. They drive their **transport trucks** day and night. They deliver loads of food to stores and restaurants. Then they carefully clean the trucks and load them up again.

Truck drivers wear masks and gloves. They are careful to not spread disease when they deliver food.

Workers carefully unload food and drinks.

SORRY I AM DIRTY
BUT WE ARE SAVING WATER!

Other workers deliver food right to people's homes. Delivery people load up cars, trucks, or bikes with food orders. Then they bring the food to people quickly and safely. Some workers even use **robots** to deliver food!

THANK YOU
TRUCK DRIVERS

Many truck drivers have worked longer hours than normal. This sign thanks them for their hard work.

Workers deliver food to people so they do not have to leave their homes.

Robots let workers deliver food without getting close to other people.

Food Scientists

Scientists study food to make sure it is safe to eat. The scientists share information and learn from each other. They have told people how to produce, cook, serve, and deliver food safely during the pandemic.

These food scientists are studying how vegetables grow.

This worker is inspecting potatoes to make sure they are safe to eat.

This scientist is studying crops on a farm.

Other food workers carefully **inspect** and test food. They visit the places where food is grown, caught, or produced. They make sure that COVID-19 is not spread in food or on food packaging.

Glossary

basic need Something that people cannot live without

disease A sickness that prevents a person's body from working as it should

groceries Food and household supplies sold at stores

inspect To look at something carefully to learn more about it or find problems with it

lockdown A rule for people to stay where they are

pandemic A disease spreading over the whole world or a very wide area, such as many countries

producer Someone who makes goods for people to buy

robot A machine that does work for people

scientists People who study and have a lot of knowledge about science

stocking up Gathering a large amount of something to use later

surface The outside or any one side of an object

transport trucks A large truck with a trailer used to bring goods from place to place

Index

About the Author

Robin Johnson is a freelance author and editor who has written more than 100 published children's books. She was fortunate to work from home during the pandemic and is grateful to all the helpers who kept her community running and her family safe.

Notes to Parents and Educators

Food Workers During COVID-19 celebrates the brave food workers who are helping members of their communities stay safe and meet their basic needs for food and water. Below are suggestions to help children make connections and develop their reading and social studies skills.

Before reading

Show children the cover of the book and read the title. Explain that food is a basic need. We need it to survive. Ask children:

- How do people meet their basic need for food? Where does your food come from?

- What jobs do food workers do?

During reading

After reading pages 8 and 9, ask children:

- How have the jobs of grocery store workers changed during COVID-19?

- Does your family get food at a grocery store? Have you seen changes at your local store?

After reading

Invite children to choose a food worker from the book. Together, create a T-Chart with columns labeled Before and After. Fill in the Before column with jobs done by the food worker before COVID-19. Then, using evidence from the book, fill in the After column with new jobs done by the food worker since the pandemic began.